# I want to be a Soldier

# I WANT TO BE A
# Soldier

**DAN LIEBMAN**

## FIREFLY BOOKS

## A FIREFLY BOOK

Published by Firefly Books Ltd. 2012

First Printing

**Publisher Cataloging-in-Publication Data (U.S.)
(Library of Congress Standards)**

Liebman, Daniel.
    I want to be a soldier/ Dan Liebman.
[24] p. : col. photos. ; cm.    I want to be.
ISBN: 978-1-77085-035-4
ISBN: 978-1-77085-036-1 (pbk.)
1. Soldiers -- Vocational guidance – Juvenile literature. I.
Title. II. Series.


355.3/3 dc22    UA25.L54  2012


**National Library of Canada Cataloguing in
Publication Data**

Liebman, Daniel
I want to be a soldier / Dan Liebman.
(I want to be)
ISBN 978-1-77085-035-4 (bound).
ISBN 978-1-77085-036-1 (pbk.).

1. Soldiers--Juvenile literature.
2. Armed Forces--Vocational guidance--Juvenile literature.
I. Title.  II. Series: I want to be

UB147.L54 2012      j355.0023      C2011-905889-8


Published in the United States by
Firefly Books (U.S.) Inc.
P.O. Box 1338, Ellicott Station
Buffalo, New York, USA,  14205

Published in Canada by
Firefly Books Ltd.
66 Leek Crescent
Richmond Hill, Ontario, L4B 1H1

**Photo Credits:**

Photos Courtesy of U.S. Army: Travis Zielinski 7;
Dalinda Hanna 11; Kim Jae-you 14; Jared Eastman 16;
Katie Summerhill 17; Robert Hyatt 18; Aaron Allman
20; Mylinda DuRousseau 21; Michael MacLeod, back
cover.

Photos Courtesy of U.S. Air Force: Susan Penning, front
cover; Bill Evans 8; Shawn Weismiller 10.

Photos Courtesy of U.S. Navy: Scott Thornbloom 9;
Alan Gragg 12; Betsy Knapper 13.

© Alan Crosthwaite/Dreamstime.com 15.
© Matt Fowler/Dreamstime.com 19.
© Tyler Stableford 22-23.
© Lauriey/Dreamstime.com 24.
© Arthur Carlo Franco Istockphoto: 5
Christian Science Monitor/Getty Images: 6.

The publisher gratefully acknowledges the financial support for our publishing program by the Government of Canada through the Canada Book Fund as administered by the Department of Canadian Heritage.

Printed in China

Recruiting offices provide information if you are thinking about becoming a soldier.

Training is important when you become a soldier. You must be in good shape.

These Air Force cadets are studying to be officers. They are looking at maps.

These students are learning how to fire a weapon safely.

This officer is finishing a six-mile march while carrying a heavy backpack.

Landing a helicopter at sea takes a lot of practice.

These sailors learn how to handle a machine gun. It's important to use equipment safely.

Officers hold important positions and need special training. Different officers hold different ranks.

Soldiers do more than fight. This soldier brought books to students.

"Open wide!" This soldier is a medic. She works with patients in a health clinic.

The Army–Navy game takes place each year between the U.S. Military Academy and the U.S. Naval Academy.

This soldier wears the famous "blue helmet" of the United Nations peacekeepers.

These soldiers are in an armored tank. They patrol a dangerous area.

Soldiers like to meet new people and help others whenever they can.

Soldiers work on the ground, on the water and in the air. If you become a soldier, what job would you like to do?

This soldier has been away from his family. It's always great to come home again.